AF583889

DEADLY SCIENCE

Renewable resources

Contents

ADJUNCT ASSOCIATE PROFESSOR COREY TUTT OAM

DEADLYSCIENCE

DeadlyScience aims to provide Science, Technology, Engineering and Mathematics (STEM) resources to remote schools around Australia. So far, DeadlyScience has shipped more than shipped more than 33,000 STEM books and resources to more than 800 schools across the country.

The organisation began when proud Kamilaroi man Corey Tutt found out that some schools in Australia were completely under-resourced and that Aboriginal and Torres Strait Islander children were discouraged from pursuing STEM because of this. DeadlyScience knows from personal experience that books and resources change lives and believes these kids deserve nothing but the best. Aboriginal and Torres Strait Islander peoples in Australia were the First Scientists of this land, and DeadlyScience is committed to preserving that history.

Renewable versus non-renewable

What is a resource? A resource is a physical material that humans need and value, such as land, air and water. Resources are materials that we need and use in everyday life. In fact, you have probably used a whole bunch of resources today without even knowing it! Resources are usually split into two groups: renewable and non-renewable. A renewable resource can replenish or replace itself at the rate it is used, while a non-renewable resource has a limited supply.

Renewable energy

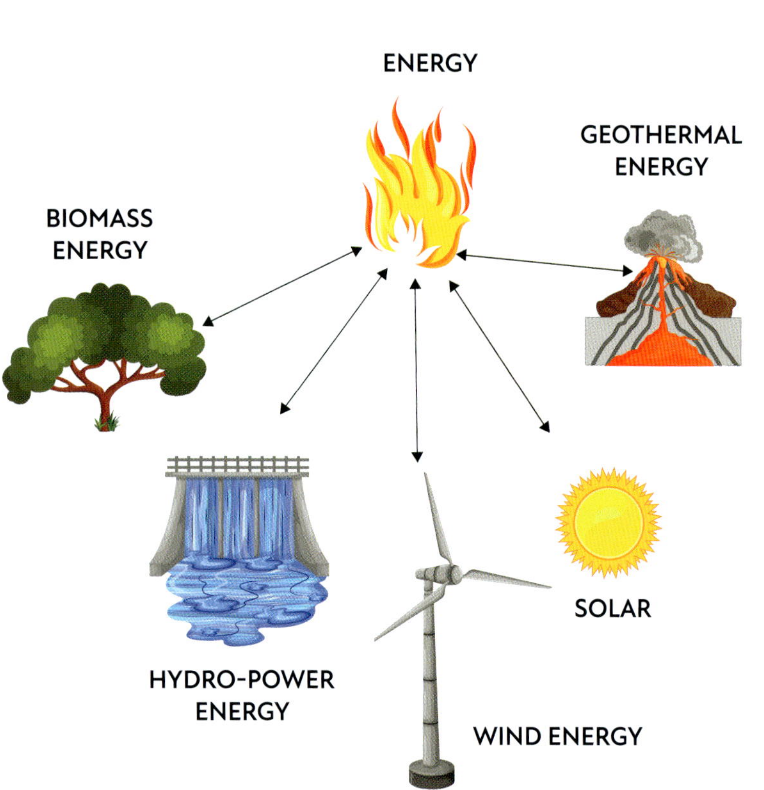

Non-renewable energy

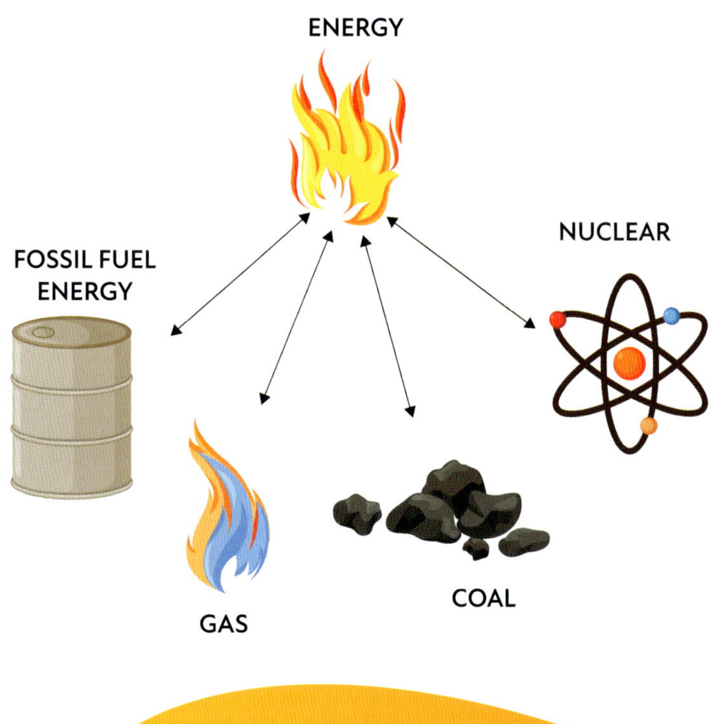

What resources do

These resources, both renewable and non-renewable, are used to create the energy that helps to power our homes, businesses and schools. This allows us to cook food, switch on the lights when it gets dark and enjoy a hot shower or bath at the end of the day. In fact, without these resources, our lives would be very different!

Coal is a non-renewable resource that is mined from the Earth.

Once upon a time...

Traditionally, non-renewable resources were our primary sources of energy. Coal, gas and oil are mined from within the Earth to be used as fuel, but they are finite resources, and once they are used up, they are gone. We also weren't always aware that these resources and practices were harmful to the Earth. This is why many people are now learning about and using renewable resources.

DID YOU KNOW?

First Nations Australians have used renewable resources like the sun for millennia. When ancient artefacts found in Central Victoria were rebuilt, they formed a clay oven that harnessed heat from the sun to slow-cook food!

Solar panels use the sun to generate renewable power.

Looking up

While only about a quarter of Australia's total energy generation is from renewable energy sources at this stage, it continues to improve, which is a shift towards a more sustainable and environmentally friendly future.

Powering Australia – renewables

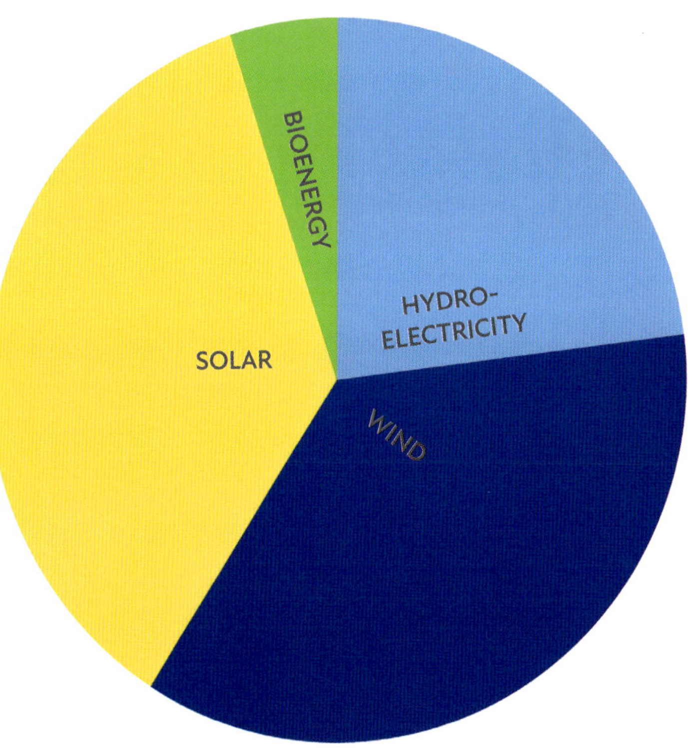

Source: Clean Energy Australia 2021.

Different types of renewable resources

Many types of renewable resources are used throughout Australia and the world. The most common are solar power, hydro-electric (water) power, geothermal energy and wind power.

Wind power

Wind power uses the energy of the wind harnessed through wind turbines, which are towers with two or three blades at the top. As the wind turns the blades, the blades turn a generator inside the tower. The internal generator creates the electricity.

Wind turbines use the wind to generate renewable power.

Solar power

Solar power comes from the sun. In a country like Australia, where we often have a lot of sunlight, solar power can be a very useful source of energy and can be harnessed via solar panels (below).

Hydro-electric power

Hydro-electric energy is generated by moving or flowing water. Most hydro-electric power plants are found in or around dams (right). Dams block a river to create a lake. A small amount of water is then forced out through tunnels in the dam. This water turns huge turbines, which generate electricity.

DID YOU KNOW?

Wind is not a new power source – far from it. The ancient Egyptians used the wind to power boats, just as Torres Strait Islander people used wind power to sail outrigger canoes, made with masts of bamboo and sails of pandanus mat, from island to island.

OUTRIGGER CANOE

Geothermal energy

Geothermal power uses the heat at the Earth's core to create energy. This is a little trickier to access than water or the sun, but it's a very effective and useful energy source.

Marine energy

Marine energy is a renewable energy source powered by the natural rise and fall of ocean tides, currents and waves. Marine energy (left) is the world's largest untapped renewable energy resource.

Across the country

In Australia, we are very lucky to have access to a variety of resources, both renewable and non-renewable. Our renewable resources are located across the different states and territories of Australia, with hydro-energy (powered by water) being the largest renewable source of power.

Small-scale efforts

Australian people have embraced renewables. By 2018, three million small-scale renewable energy systems had been installed. One in five homes generated renewable energy and reduced carbon emissions through rooftop solar, while others had solar water heaters and air source heat pumps. The number is even higher today.

Source: Australian Government Clean Energy Regulator 2018.

Wind and sun

Wind and solar power are becoming more popular as a source of renewable energy for large scale projects, too. Wind and solar farms can be found throughout Australia. Queensland's Coopers Gap Wind Farm produces enough megawatts to power about 264,000 homes! And in 2021, New South Wales invested $5600 million into large-scale renewable energy projects.

FACT

There are more than 120 operating hydro-electric plants in Australia. Most of them are in states that have high rainfall, such as NSW and Tasmania.

Tasmania's Gordon Dam powers the Gordon Power Station.

Power of the tides

Tidal energy, a form of marine energy, is power produced by the natural rise and fall of tides. The western and southern coastlines of Australia, especially Tasmania and the north-west coast of Western Australia, have our strongest tides, and these places are part of many ongoing projects to work out whether tidal energy could play a more important role as a power source.

Beneath the surface

Australia also has geothermal energy sources. Special geothermal systems are used to pull the Earth's heat out of 'hot rocks' (huge granite slabs beneath the Earth's surface) or from within subterranean liquids. The majority of Australia's geothermal energy can be found in South Australia, Victoria and Western Australia.

First Nations Brewarrina Fish Traps, near Barwon, NSW.

DID YOU KNOW?

Aboriginal and Torres Strait Islander peoples have long known the power of the tides; those living on the coast linked lunar phases to the tides and used the tides to wash fish into cleverly made traps.

Geothermal energy

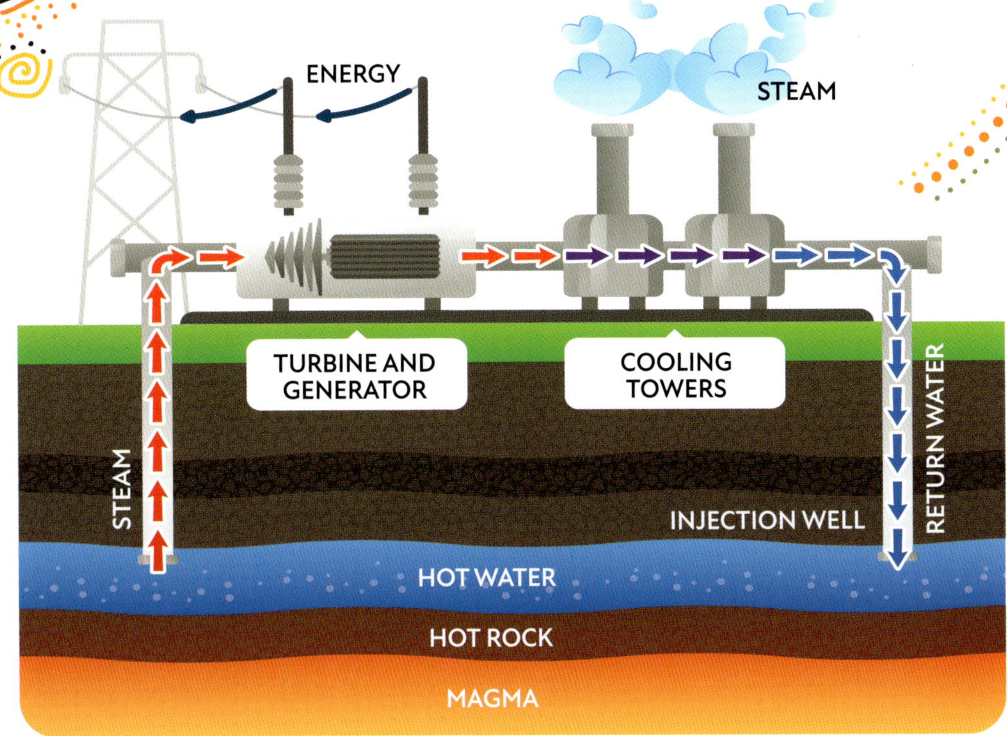

Non-renewable energy

Most of Australia's energy comes from non-renewable resources, mainly from sources that are known as fossil fuels. You might know these as coal, petroleum (or oil), and natural gas.

What is fossil fuel?

Fossil fuel is very, very old. Hundreds of millions of years old, to be exact! Back then, the Earth's surface was very different. Instead of being home to humans and animals, it was covered in water, from both the sea and from swamps and ponds. Plants, algae and plankton thrived in this environment. They would absorb sunlight and then turn this sunlight into energy through photosynthesis.

When they died, these organisms ended up under water, but they'd still have their stash of energy. As our Earth evolved, these dead organisms fell to the bottom, with rocks, sediment and even the sea on top of them. This created a lot of heat and pressure until these remains eventually turned into fossil fuel. Today, huge pockets of these resources remain below the Earth's surface, but once they are extracted and used, they will be gone.

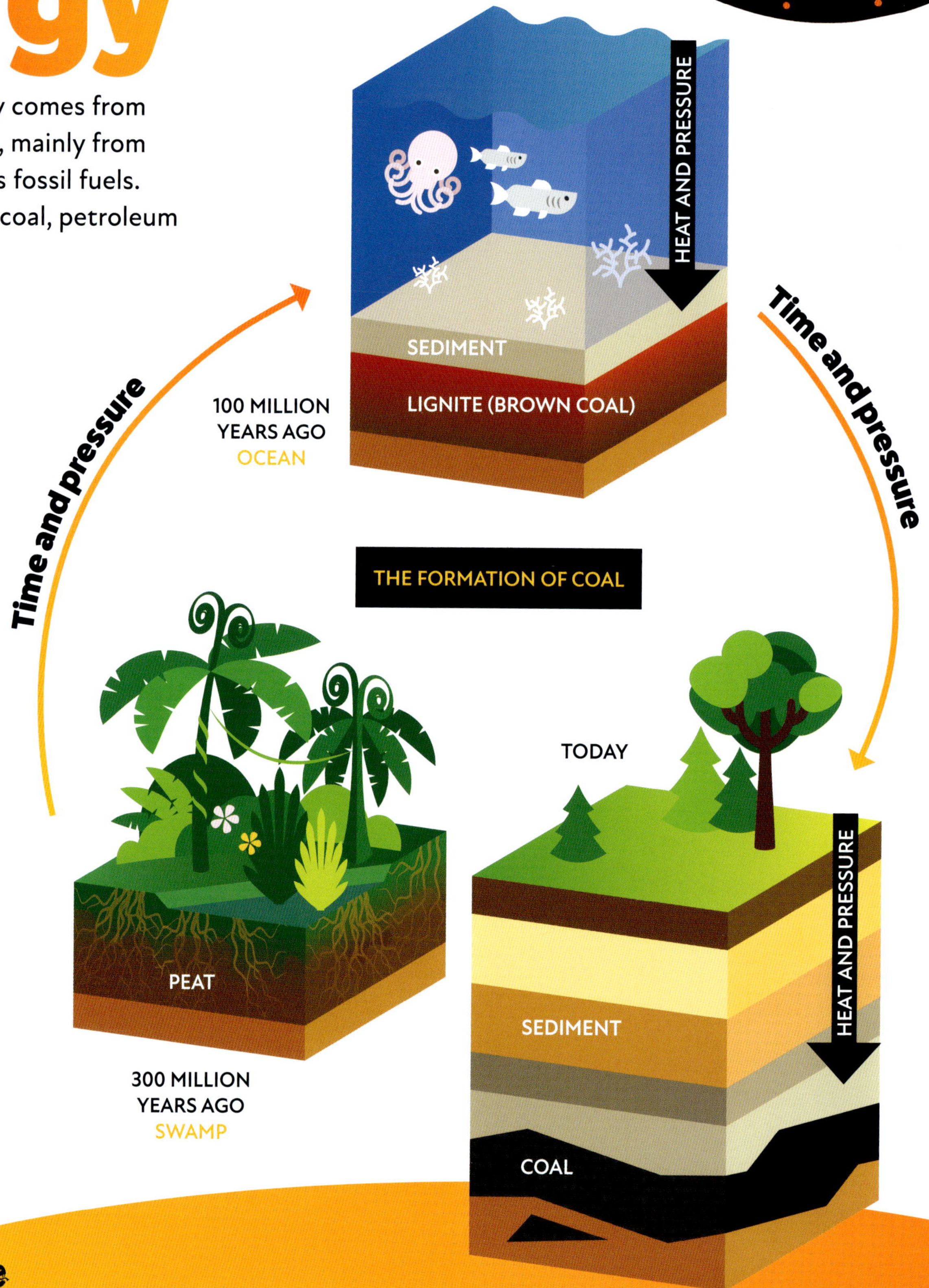

THE FORMATION OF COAL

100 MILLION YEARS AGO
OCEAN

HEAT AND PRESSURE

SEDIMENT

LIGNITE (BROWN COAL)

Time and pressure

TODAY

HEAT AND PRESSURE

SEDIMENT

COAL

Time and pressure

300 MILLION YEARS AGO
SWAMP

PEAT

How do we turn fossil fuel into energy?

To access fossil fuel, we need to drill down into the Earth to mine whichever fuel we're looking for. Once we've found it, we then need to extract it by using various mining techniques, which often have a negative impact on the health of our planet. Once we've managed to extract the fuel, it is then burnt to create the energy we need. When coal and oil are burnt, they release a gas called carbon dioxide.

Carbon dioxide traps heat within the Earth's atmosphere. It can also pollute the air, water and land and contribute to the 'greenhouse effect', which results in global warming.

A coal-powered electrical station

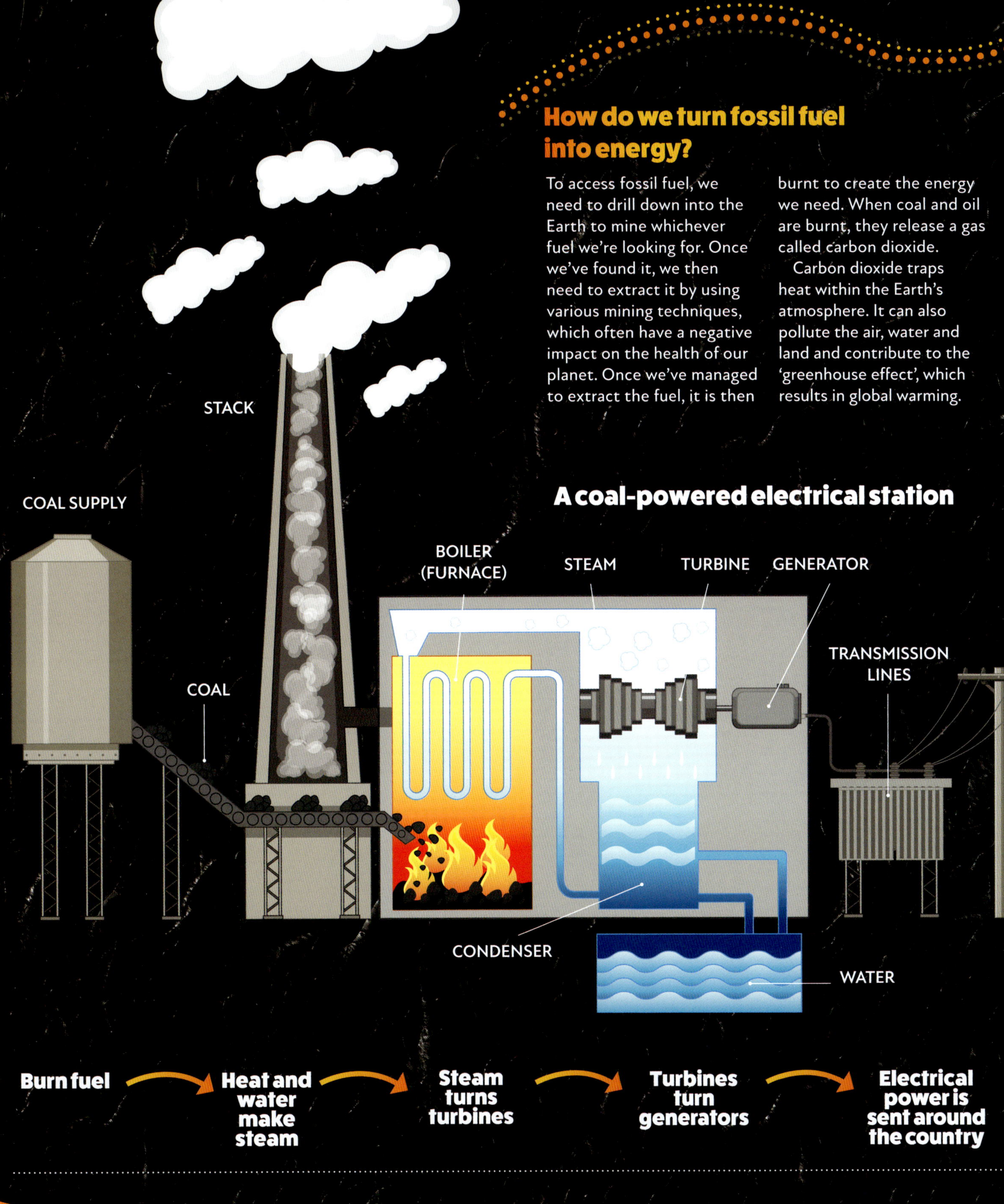

Burn fuel → **Heat and water make steam** → **Steam turns turbines** → **Turbines turn generators** → **Electrical power is sent around the country**

The greenhouse effect and climate change

The greenhouse effect is a natural process that warms the Earth's surface. When the sun's very hot rays reach our atmosphere, some rays bounce back into space while the rest are absorbed by the earth and the ocean, heating both. This heat then radiates from our planet to space. Some of this heat is trapped by greenhouse gases. This process has kept the Earth warm enough to sustain life, but human activities can disrupt the balance, leading to climate change.

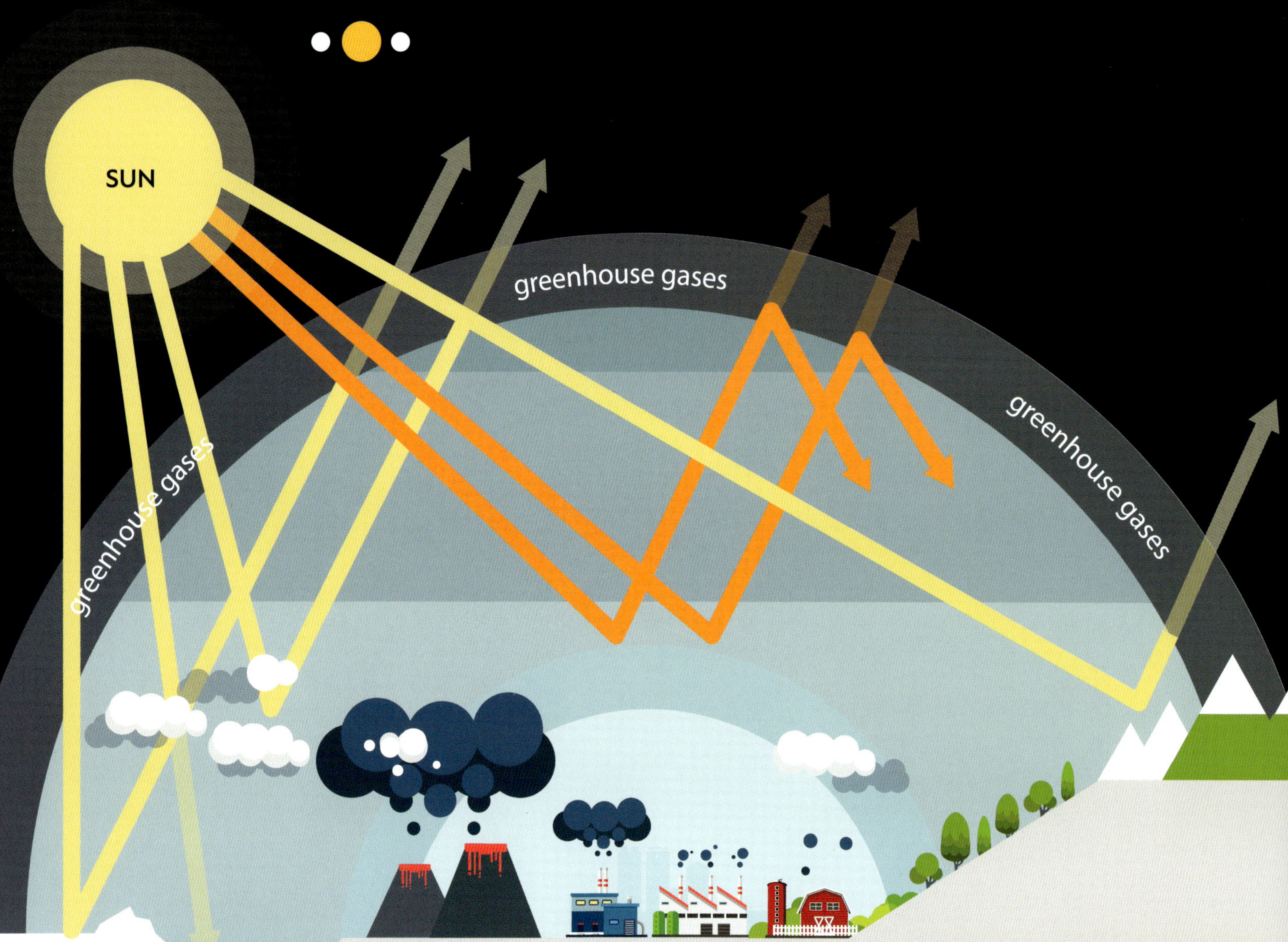

Bana is the word for rain in the Djabugay language of the Cairns region in Queensland.

FLOODS

A big problem

The Earth's climate changes over time for many different reasons; however, many scientists agree that over the past 50–100 years, human activity has been a major factor. That is because burning fossil fuels has increased greenhouse gases, which, in turn, warms the Earth and changes the climate.

DID YOU KNOW?

In Australia, we have experienced an increase of nearly 1 °C in our annual temperatures. That might not sound like a lot, but it shows that warming is occurring at TWICE the rate it was. This may increase weather phenomena, such as extreme heat, bushfires, droughts and floods.

MELTING ICE

Why it is a problem

Our planet is getting hotter. And while we all enjoy staying warm, an increase in Earth's temperature isn't a good thing. Climate change refers to things such as increased air and ocean temperatures, which result in rising sea levels, melting snow and ice, drought, floods, and dangerous changes in weather and rainfall.

5 fast facts about the greenhouse effect

1. Greenhouse gases include carbon dioxide, methane, nitrous oxide, ozone, water vapour and some artificial chemicals.
2. The greenhouse effect is a natural and necessary process, but some of our activities lead to more gas being produced.
3. If we didn't have any greenhouse gases, the Earth's temperature would be -18 °C. Brrrrr! That is way too cold to sustain life.
4. Burning fossil fuels for energy results in extra greenhouse gases being released into the atmosphere.
5. Renewable energy sources can provide energy without the planet-warming effects of fossil fuels. This is why renewable resources are sometimes referred to as 'clean energy'.

Solar energy

Solar energy is one of the most popular renewable resources in Australia due to the amount of sunlight available! If you've ever been outside on a hot summer's day, you'll know how strong the sun can be. Solar power takes this energy from the sun and converts it into electricity we can use. Solar power can also heat air, water or other substances. In Australia, solar power comes from two main sources: solar panels installed in homes and businesses, and solar farms.

How solar energy works

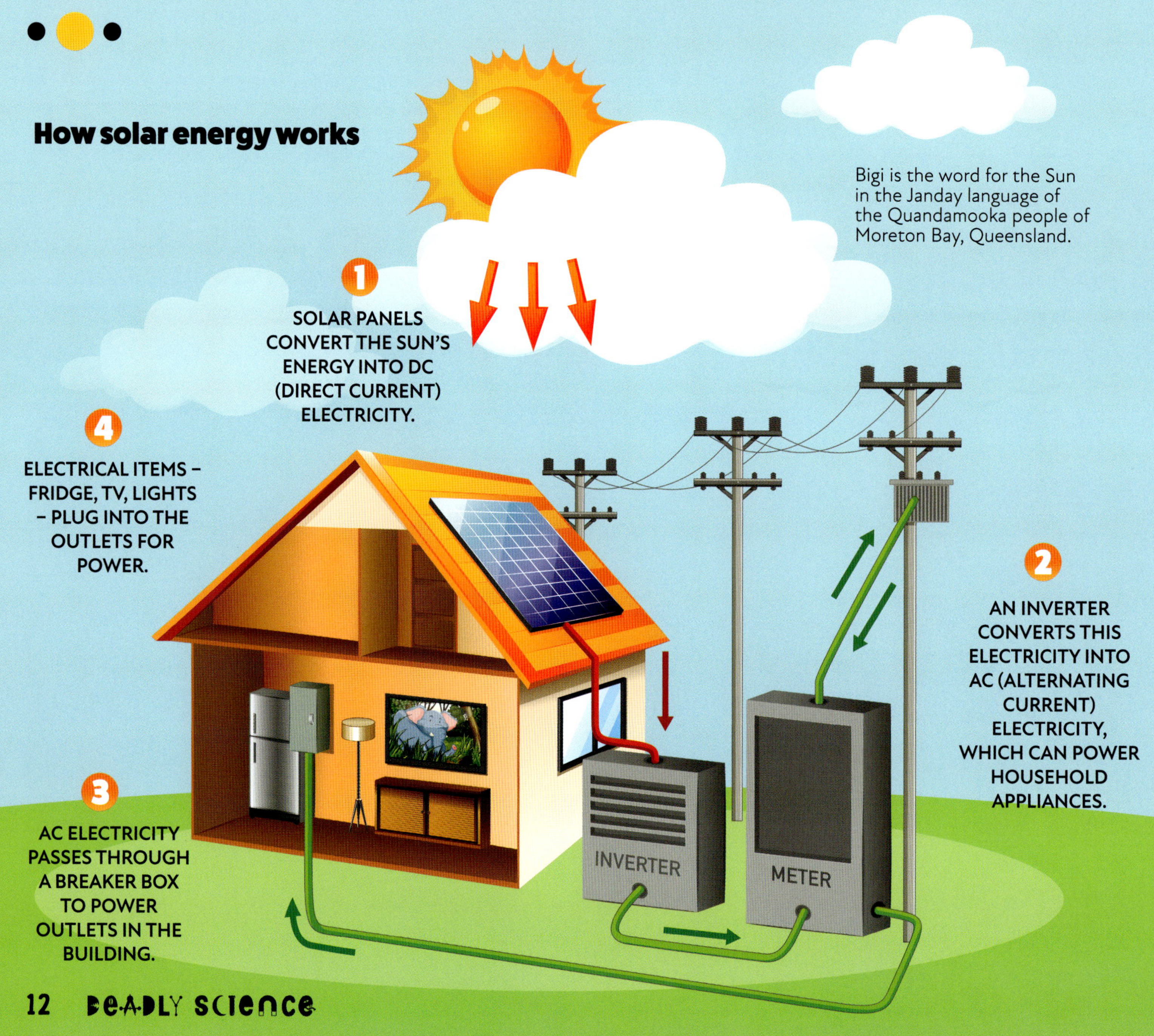

Bigi is the word for the Sun in the Janday language of the Quandamooka people of Moreton Bay, Queensland.

Solar panels are increasingly powering homes and businesses, which reduces electricity costs and emissions.

Solar in our homes and businesses

If you go outside and have a look around, you may notice a few (or maybe more) houses around you with solar panels attached to the roof. These panels contain a special kind of technology called 'solar photovoltaic' or 'solar PV', which converts sunlight into electricity. This electricity is then used to power homes and businesses. It is a very useful and renewable source of power, especially in our Australian climate.

DID YOU KNOW?

The Australian continent has the HIGHEST solar radiation (that is, sunlight) per m² of any continent in the world.

Solar for our water

Energy from the sun can also be converted to heat, which is known as 'thermal energy'. This can then be used to drive electricity generators, which provide a source of power for different things throughout homes and businesses, from heating (right) to computer servers. One of the most popular uses of thermal energy is in solar hot water systems. This works by storing energy from the sun in the form of hot water, which then sits in the hot water tank, ready to be used when you need a hot shower or to do the washing up!

Solar farms

Solar farms are a popular renewable energy source. They use the same technology used in homes and businesses, but on a much bigger scale. Think thousands of solar panels, all harvesting energy from the sun! Many solar farms are already operating, with more under construction.

Western Downs Green Power Hub in Queensland, and Darlington Point Solar Farm in NSW are two of the largest solar farms, each with more than one million solar panels that generate enough electricity to power more than 100,000 homes and businesses.

FACT

***Vanguard I*, the first artificial satellite powered by solar energy, has travelled more than 9 billion km.**

Try this fun experiment to learn about the Sun's power.

LEARNING TASK

Solar in action

Ever wondered just how powerful the sun really is? Try this easy experiment!

What you'll need

- 3 plastic cups, all the same size
- 3 pieces of paper or cardboard, one white, one yellow (or another pale colour) and one black
- 1 piece of plastic cling wrap
- Measuring cup
- Thermometer
- Cool water

What to do

STEP 1
Choose a warm spot with plenty of sunlight.

STEP 2
Measure the same amount of water into each of the cups.

STEP 3
Place each cup on a different piece of paper.

STEP 4
Record the temperature of the water in each cup.

STEP 5
Cover the cup on the white or pale paper with plastic wrap.

STEP 6
Leave in the sun for 1–2 hours.

STEP 7
Remove the plastic wrap and record the temperature of water in each cup.

Questions

- Which is the warmest?
- Why do you think this is?
- Why do you think we used different coloured paper?

Rank the different cups from warmest to coolest.

- What else could utilise the sun's energy for heating and cooling?

Geothermal energy

The centre, or core, of the Earth is extremely hot – more than 6000 °C in some parts! Scientists have worked out how to make use of this heat, which is called geothermal energy.

Hot rocks

Geothermal energy is stored in granite rocks or trapped in liquids, such as water. Getting energy from the Earth is a similar process to what is used to access fossil fuels – drilling and wells. Miners drill into the ground to find hot rocks or reservoirs of hot water. Water is then pumped in, and it rapidly heats up. This water is then pushed back to the surface where the heat turns a turbine that produces electricity.

MATARANKA HOT SPRINGS, NT

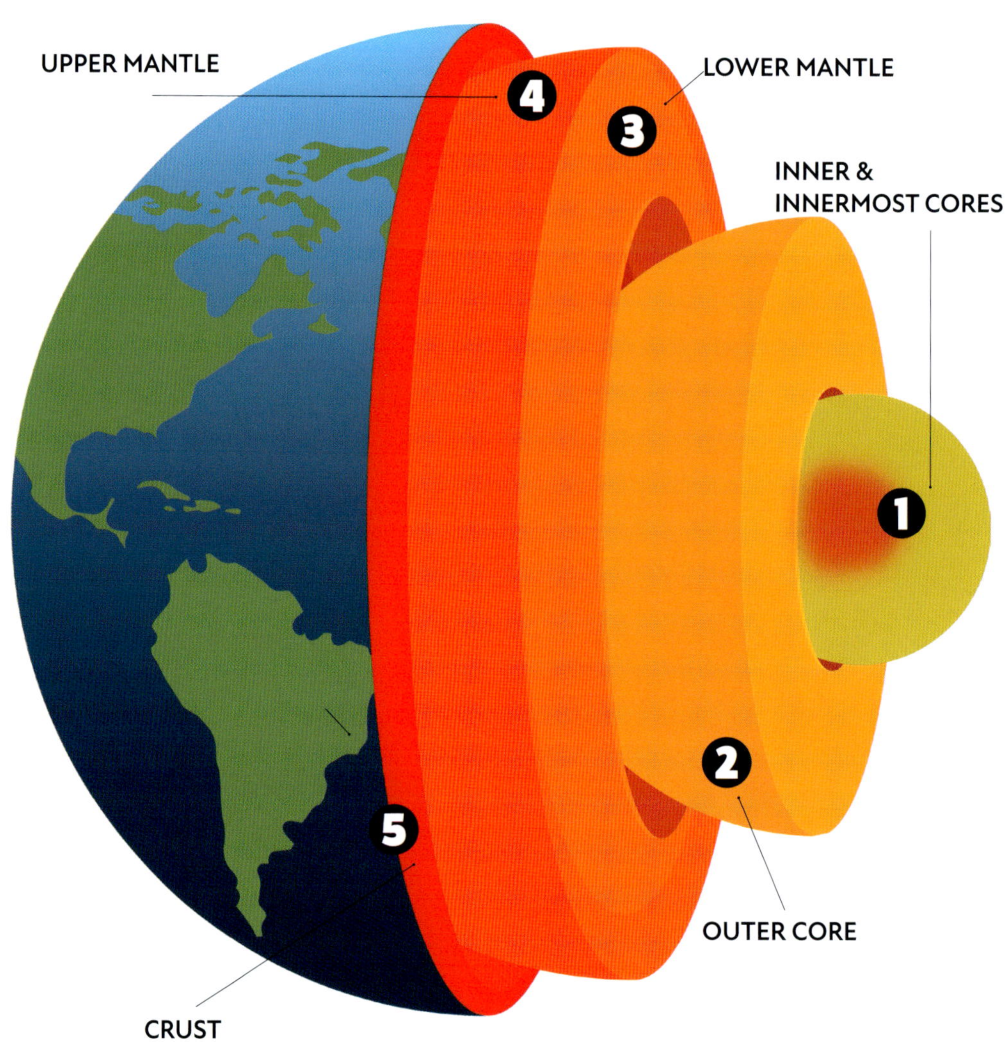

1 Inner and innermost cores
The innermost core is the hottest layer. Amazingly, the inner and innermost cores don't melt, due to pressure from above.

2 Outer core
The liquid outer core is made up of a band of 2200 km thick iron and nickel.

3 Lower mantle
Also known as the mesosphere, the lower mantle consists of hot rock (4000 °C) under enormous pressure.

4 Upper mantle
This largely solid rock is up to 640 km thick and can flow over long periods of time.

5 Crust
The crust is 5 km thick under the oceans and 70 km thick beneath the continents.

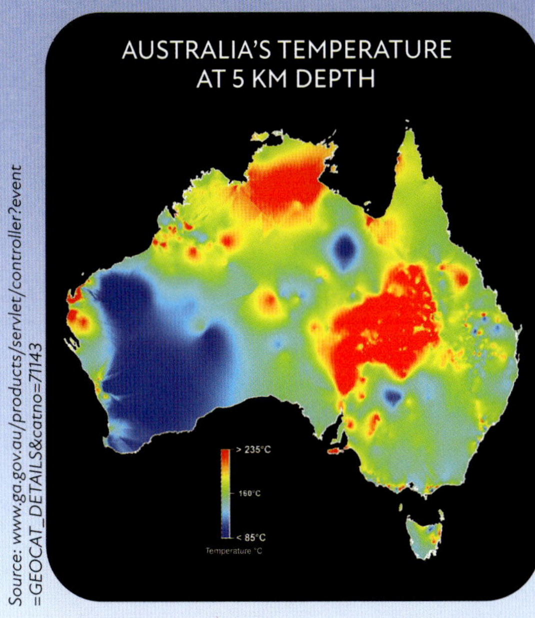

Source: www.ga.gov.au/products/servlet/controller?event=GEOCAT_DETAILS&catno=71143

Geothermal energy in Australia

While Australia has a lot of geothermal energy potential, it is still in the early stages of being used as an energy source. This is because the reserves of geothermal energy are in very isolated areas, making it difficult to mine or use for power. It's a renewable resource that is a key focus for many sustainable energy groups as they work out how they might be able to make it work in Australia.

FACT

Iceland gets almost 100% of its energy from renewable sources, including hydro-power and geothermal energy.

DID YOU KNOW?

First Nations peoples have been using geothermal energy, in the form of hot springs and pools for bathing and cooking, for tens of thousands of years!

Iceland uses almost 100% renewables for power – 73% hydro-electricity and almost 27% geothermal.

Wind power

Wind power is one of the oldest sources of energy, from sails to windmills, although we've made some improvements to it in our modern age. Today, we use wind turbines. You might have seen them if you've driven through an area with a wind farm.

Yawi is the word for wind in the Gunggay language of Far North Queensland.

How does wind create electricity?

Wind turbines have two or three blades, which are turned by the wind. As the blades turn, they power a generator inside the turbine. This generator then creates electricity, which is stored or exported to the grid. To generate the amount of electricity needed to power homes and businesses, wind turbines are grouped together to create wind farms.

BLADE

TRANSMISSION GEAR

CONTROLLER

WIRES TO TRANSFER ELECTRICITY

GENERATOR

BRAKE

YAW MOTOR

TOWER

FACT

While wind turbines look simple from the outside, they are quite complex inside. Each one contains about 8000 parts.

New South Wales has several wind farms, including this one near Bungendore on the traditional lands of the Ngarigo people.

Wind power in Australia

Wind power is one of Australia's main sources of renewable energy, with more than 100 wind farms currently operating across the country and more being constructed. Wind power is a cheap and effective source of energy, which is one of the reasons it is so valuable to Australia.

New technology means that wind turbines are getting bigger, stronger and more efficient, which will lead to more energy being generated by fewer turbines. Wind power is even being used in some homes, where an individual home turbine is installed to generate power. Landowners who have a large enough plot of land can also install wind turbines for their own use.

DID YOU KNOW?

Some countries locate their wind turbines in the ocean! They either float on the surface of the water or sit on extra-long pylons that extend up from the seabed.

Wind power in remote Indigenous communities

The Aboriginal community of Gawa on Elcho Island, almost 550 km east of Darwin in the Northern Territory, has installed a wind turbine in the school to help replace the diesel generator currently used to power the community. The generator would cut out up to 64 times a day, cost about $80,000 a year to run, and was not a clean energy option. It is thought that this may be the most remote wind turbine in Australia.

Hydro-electric power

Hydro-electric power is a form of renewable energy that uses moving water, usually from a constructed dam, to spin a turbine connected to a generator. This, in turn, creates electricity.

Power of water

Hydro-electricity is a popular renewable resource in Australia, with a growing number of hydro-electric plants operating throughout the country. These plants produce about a quarter of the total clean renewable energy generated in Australia.

Hydro-electric power plant

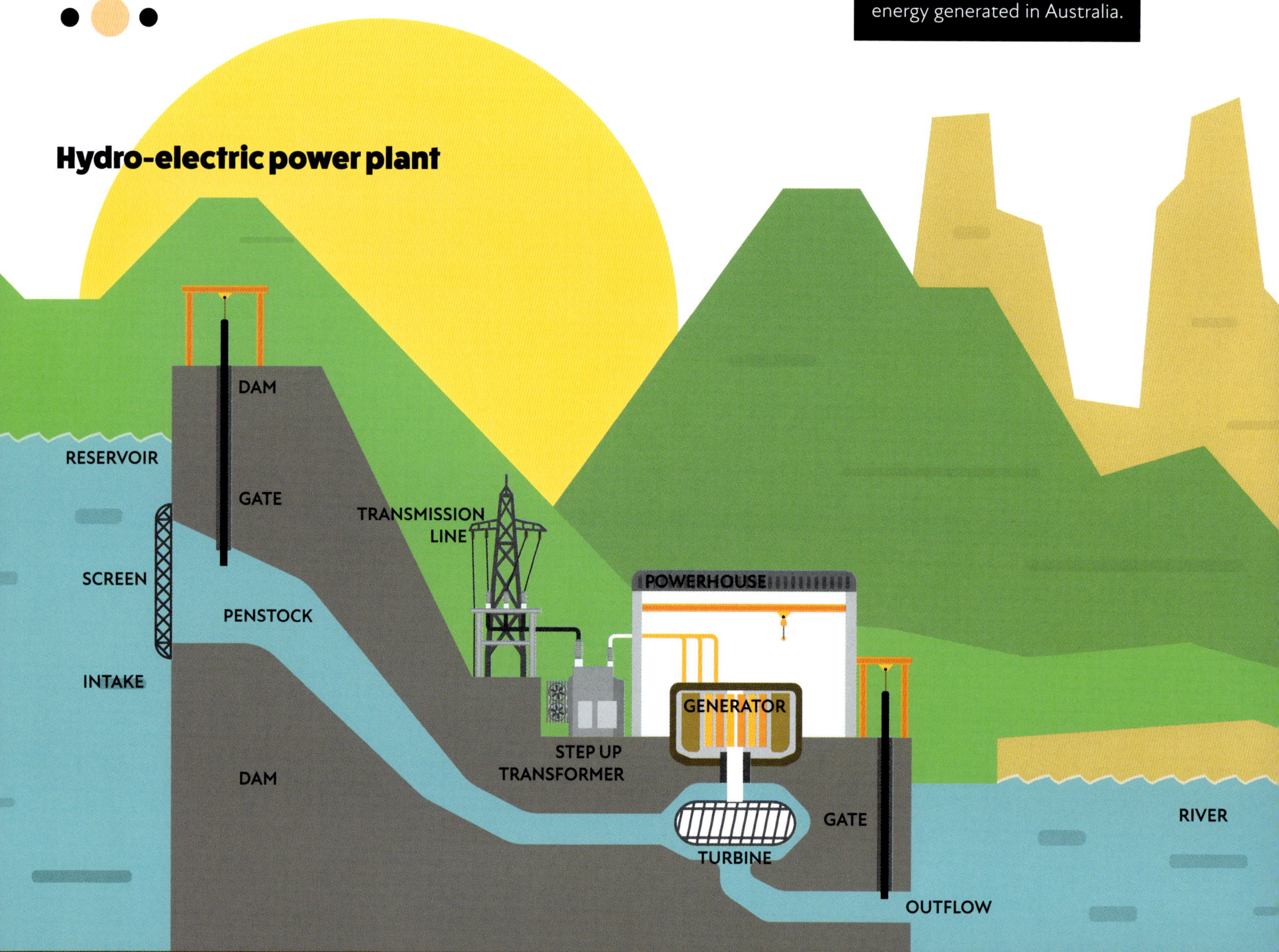

The different types of plants

There are three types of hydro-electric plants. One uses a dam to control the flow of water. Another uses canals to channel flowing river water towards the turbines. A third collects the energy produced from solar and wind and stores it by pumping water up to another reservoir to then allow this water to flow back down to a lower reservoir and turn the turbine when needed.

Tarraleah Power Station, one of Hydro Tasmania's many renewables projects.

DID YOU KNOW?

Hydro Tasmania is located in the middle of Tasmania and consists of 52 lakes, 54 large dams, 30 hydro-power stations and some wind farms. Hydro Tasmania generates enough energy to power more than 900,000 homes. That's a lot of water!

Rain power

Hydro-electricity is a great renewable resource, as it is clean and effective, although the amount of power generated is determined by the amount of rainfall. That is why the majority of hydro-electric plants are found in areas that get rain more regularly, such as Tasmania and New Zealand (left). You wouldn't find one in the middle of the desert!

More than 2000 years ago, people in Greece used flowing water to turn the wheels of their mills to grind wheat into flour.

Marine energy

Marine energy is one of the newer renewable energy sources being explored in Australia. It uses the rise and fall of ocean tides and currents, waves, and even the changing temperature of the ocean, along with turbines and paddles, to generate electricity. Three types of marine energy can be used to generate power: wave, tidal, and ocean thermal energy.

A power plant uses tidal energy to produce electricity.

FACT

A CSIRO study showed that wave energy could produce up to 11% of Australia's power needs by 2050.

DID YOU KNOW?

Marine energy is renewable because the Moon controls the tides, the wind creates waves, and the Sun heats up the oceans.

Wave energy

Australia is home to some very large waves, especially along our southern coastline. Wave power plants use the energy from the up and down tumble of waves and convert it to electricity!

An Australian company called Wave Swell Energy is currently working on a project to harness the power of the waves using a special generator that will be anchored to the sea floor near the coast of King Island, an island in Bass Strait between Victoria and Tasmania, which often has a lot of very large waves.

Meerteeyt is a word for sea in the Gunditjmara language of Victoria.

Tidal energy

You might have been at the beach at high or low tide before. Tides cause movement of the water and can be very strong and powerful. To harness this, a special turbine (similar to a wind turbine) is connected to a gearbox and generator. As the turbine rotates in the tide, it switches on the gearbox. This then powers the generator and creates electricity. Tidal energy is in its infancy and is still being explored in Australia, but it is hoped that it will become a useful renewable resource.

Tidal currents can be harnessed to generate clean, green electricity.

Wave energy

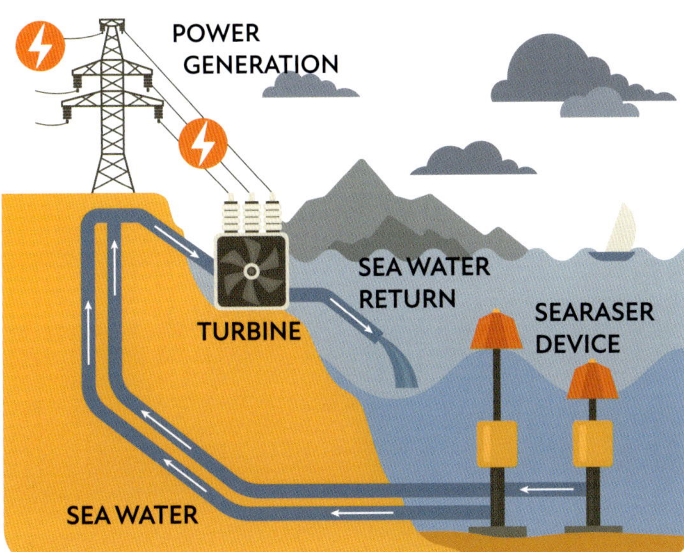

Ocean thermal energy

Ocean thermal energy is a little bit different, as it uses the temperature changes in the ocean to generate electricity. You might have noticed when swimming in the ocean that the water at the surface can be quite warm, but the deeper you go, the colder the water gets. Ocean thermal energy uses that difference in temperature to extract energy.

At the moment, ocean thermal energy is not being used in Australia as a source of energy, but it is being investigated for possible use in the future.

Renewable resources around the world

Renewable energy sources are a hot topic of conversation around the world. Many countries are committed to switching to renewable resources for power.

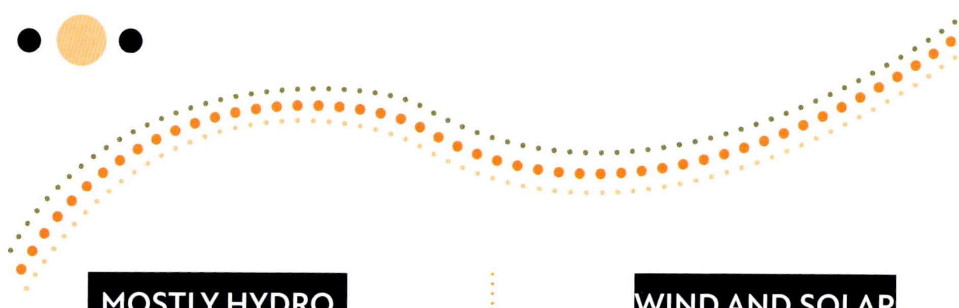

Clean and green

In 2021, Norway, New Zealand and Brazil were generating the highest share of renewable energy. New Zealand, which aims to be using 100% renewables by 2035, takes advantage of the fact that it sits in the path of the winds known as the Roaring Forties. These are very strong westerly winds created by warm air rising near the Equator and moving towards the South Pole. Australia also has these winds.

MOSTLY HYDRO

Norway
more than
98%
of electricity supply

WIND AND SOLAR

New Zealand
more than
80%
of electricity supply

BIOFUELS AND WASTE

Brazil
more than
78%
of electricity supply

Source: Enerdata 2021 and Climate Council 2022.

DID YOU KNOW?

After a wind turbine is installed, all it needs to keep producing electricity is a little maintenance from time to time. It doesn't need someone to find new wind for it to make electricity.

Other countries making a real difference

Uruguay

According to the International Trade Administration, Uruguay currently generates more than 98% of its electricity from renewable sources, primarily wind and hydro-power.

Sweden

Sweden has set a very ambitious goal to be completely fossil fuel-free by 2045, with all of their electricity generated by other sources. Currently, they are on track to achieve it.

Germany

Germany has set a target of 80% renewable power by 2030. And thanks to wind, biomass, solar and hydropower, it produces enough renewable energy to power every house in the country.

Scotland

Scotland has dedicated itself to wind power in a big way! Renewables now generate almost 100% of the country's electricity needs, thanks to the world's largest floating wind farm off their coast.

Iceland

Iceland is one of the few countries that runs on almost 100% renewable energy, thanks to hydro and geothermal energy from the country's many active volcanoes and geysers.

Morocco

Home to the world's biggest concentrated solar power plant, Morocco's Noor Ouarzazate Solar Complex provides half of Morocco's electricity needs.

Denmark

Denmark set a world record in 2017 by getting more than half its electricity from wind power. Wind generated 43% of its electricity, the highest of any OECD country, while bioenergy supplied 66% of its renewable energy, and solar did its bit too. It aims to be 100% fossil fuel-free by 2050.

Costa Rica

It may be small – with a population of just over 5 million, compared to our more than 25 million! – but Costa Rica is committed to changing the planet for the better. Renewable sources, including hydro, geothermal, solar and wind power, have generated 98% of their energy for seven years in a row.

Case study: coal and its impact on the Australian environment

Australia still gets the majority of its energy from non-renewable fossil fuels – coal, oil and natural gas.

How does coal impact the environment?

Coal is a valuable resource in Australia, but it is one that causes problems for our health and the environment. Mining coal and burning it for electricity is the largest contributor to climate pollution in Australia. It impacts the air we breathe, the land we live on and the water we use.

Mining has a huge impact on the environment; it involves tearing up large sections of land, destroying the plants and displacing the animals that lived there. When the minerals run out, the land is left useless, contaminated and stripped of nutrients. It can lead to the breakdown of various natural features and result in the removal of trees, plants and wildlife. It can also cause what is referred to as degradation, or destruction, of the surrounding soil.

Mining destroys the land and eradicates plants and animals.

Jabiluka: mining for power on Indigenous sacred sites

Mining has a long-running and significant impact on Indigenous land and sacred sites. Jabiluka, in the Northern Territory, has deposits of uranium, which is a valuable heavy metal. But this land belongs to the Mirrar clan of Aboriginal people, who have called it home for tens of thousands of years. The area contains artefacts, rock art and Dreamtime connections for the Mirrar people. After uranium was discovered there in 1971, drilling began, and a plan was proposed for a mine to be built. However, the Traditional Owners, who wanted to protect their land and sacred sites, weren't consulted on this decision. After much disappointment was expressed throughout Australia, the plan to mine was changed, and the land began to be rehabilitated and restored.

Coal mining in Australia

0 750km

DARWIN
LAURA BASIN
CANNING BASIN
NT
QLD
GALILEE BASIN
BOWEN BASIN
STYX BASIN
CALLIDE BASIN
MULGIDIE BASIN
MARYBOROUGH BASIN
TARONG BASIN
BRISBANE
IPSWICH BASIN
CLARENCE–MORETON BASIN
WA
ARCKARINGA BASIN
SA
SURAT BASIN
PERTH BASIN
EUCLA BASIN
LEIGH CREEK
GUNNEDAH BASIN
GLOUCESTER BASIN
PERTH
POLDA BASIN
MURRAY BASIN
NSW
SYDNEY
SYDNEY BASIN
COLLIE BASIN
SAINT VINCENT BASIN
ACT
CANBERRA
ADELAIDE
OAKLANDS BASIN
VIC
MELBOURNE
OTWAY BASIN
GIPPSLAND BASIN
LONGFORD BASIN
TAS
TASMANIA BASIN
HOBART

Recoverable black and brown coal resources

- Black coal basin
- Brown coal basin
- Black coal operating mine
- Brown coal operating mine
- Black coal mineral deposit
- Brown coal mineral deposit

Source: Geoscience Australia 2017.

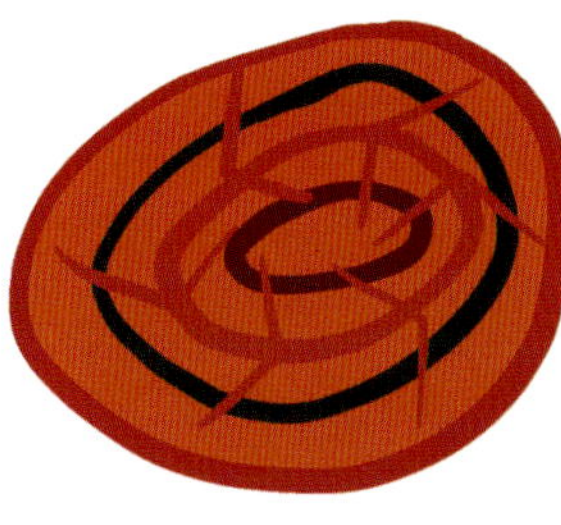

Australia's statistics

Primary energy refers to the raw materials that produce energy, such as coal, gas, wind or water. Electricity is one of the things we make from those raw materials. Approximately 70% of Australia's primary energy comes from coal and gas.

Australia is the largest exporter of coal in the world. We mine coal and send it to other countries for them to use. Many coal mines operate all over Australia, to find and extract this coal to use here as well as to send it overseas, primarily to eastern Asian countries.

Solar farms in space!

We've learnt all about solar power and how this renewable resource can be used to generate huge amounts of energy, but that was all based on Earth! Space-based solar would use inflatable modules with mirrors that could be sent into orbit and direct sunlight onto solar panels. This energy would then be sent back down to Earth. Exciting, isn't it?

NASA's solar power satellites (SPS) concept for solar power.

Renewable resources of the future

Lots of renewable resources are currently being used in Australia and around the world. While they'll continue to be developed, here are a few futuristic renewable resource ideas that just might end up becoming part of the energy production of tomorrow.

Human power

Could you power your house just by walking? Scientists believe that in the not-too-distant future we will be able to harness our daily movement to create power. To make this work, we'd have to wear a system that would collect and convert our movement into usable energy. How this could work is still being studied, but with over 7 billion people walking each day, it's a nifty idea!

People power (top), and powered by pigs!

Poo power

Can poo be turned into energy? It seems it can, at least in Kenya! Special bio-centres have been set up to collect human poo, which is then put into a special machine where a gas called methane is extracted. This gas is collected and can then be used to heat the water for showers, and even to heat up the oven! Kenya isn't the only country keen to see what poo can do. A pig farm in Australia recently began converting the huge amounts of pig poop they had into renewable electricity, using a special methane digestion system. This system captures the methane gas from the pig poo and turns it into electricity!

DID YOU KNOW?

Research is being done to see if solar wind (streams of energised particles from the sun) can be harnessed to create power.

Work up a sweat for a good cause.

Sweat power

Similar to human power, sweat power would use sweat to power small devices, such as smartwatches and phones! Researchers in Tokyo were able to create a special cell that turned sweat into electricity. They did this by using the electrochemical reaction between something called lactate (which is found in sweat) and a special enzyme. This reaction produced a current that was collected and transferred. Isn't that amazing?

Precious water

We challenge you to complete this resource activity and help the planet at the same time!

Water is one of the world's most precious resources. Every day in Australia, we use on average a whopping 340 L per person. That's a lot of water! We can save a great deal of it by paying attention to how we use it. Did you know that Indigenous Australians were very good at this? It makes sense, seeing as our continent is one of the driest places in the world! They created underground water reservoirs and even used filters to make the water clean to drink.

Old-style shower heads can use 15–20 L of water per minute. Use a timer to limit your showers to 3–4 minutes.

FACT

Kamilaroi people used a shallow dish called a coolamon, made from wood, woven material or hide, to carry water.

What to do

1. Keep a diary record of the water you and your family use for a week.
2. Now, calculate how much water you have used. Every minute of running a tap is 6 L; a dishwasher uses 13 L per load; depending on your washing machine, a two-star 6 kg machine uses 130 L per load, while a four-star uses 60 L–71 L per load. Some food for thought – if you turn off the tap while brushing your teeth and use a glass of water instead, you can save a whopping 18 L of water each time!
3. Share this information with your family. The second week, do everything you can to sensibly reduce your water use.
4. Do a second calculation.
5. Challenge your friends and family to do the same. It'll change the way you use water forever.

Hardie Grant acknowledges the Traditional Owners of the Country on which we work, the Wurundjeri People of the Kulin Nation and the Gadigal People of the Eora Nation, and recognises their continuing connection to the land, waters and culture. We pay our respects to their Elders past and present.

Hardie Grant Children's Publishing
Wurundjeri Country
Level 11, 36 Wellington Street
Collingwood Victoria 3066
Melbourne | Sydney | San Francisco
hardiegrant.com/childrens
www.australiangeographic.com.au
ISBN: 9781761216640
First published 2022
This edition published 2025

Series editor Corey Tutt **Illustrator** Mim Cole / Mimmim
Author Naomi Foxall **Designer** Harmony Southern

Publisher Penelope White **Editor** Savannah Hollis with Olivia Brown
Cover design Andy Warren **Internal design** Hannah Janzen
Production Sally Davis

Printed in China by LEO Paper Products LTD

The paper this book is printed on is from FSC® certified forests and other controlled sources. FSC® promotes environmentally responsible, socially beneficial and economically viable management of the world's forests.

10 9 8 7 6 5 4 3 2 1

A catalogue record for this book is available from the National Library of Australia

Picture credits

Front Cover: Illustrations Mim Cole; Clockwise from top left: James Parascandola/Shutterstock; Ponkrit/SS; EsHanPhot/SS; esbobeldijk/SS; Diane Diederich/SS; lomiso/SS; Todd S. Holder/SS. **1:** Corey Tutt; **2:** Vecton/SS. **3:** Mim Cole; Australian Geographic; Vyacheslav Svetlichnyy/SS; myphotobank.com.au/SS. **4:** kwest/SS.**5:** Mim Cole; Adwo/SS; art-siberia/SS; Johann Ragnarsson/SS; Breedfoto/SS; AlfradHaddon 1888/Public Domain. **6:** boreala/SS. **7:** crbellette/SS; VectorMine/SS; John Carnemolla/SS. **8:** VectorMine/SS. **9:** BlueRingMedia/SS. **10:** trgrowth/SS. **11:** Johan Larson/SS; Jan Miko/SS; JP Phillippe/SS. **12:** BlueRingMedia/SS. **13:** Adam Calaitzis/SS; Mariia Boiko/SS. **14:** Steve Tritton/SS. **15:** PaniYani/SS; kristnu/SS. **16:** FoxGrafy/SS; Bynker/SS. **17:** Geoscience Australia; Ondrej Bucek/SS. **18:** TatyanaTVK/SS. **19:** Steve Tritton/SS; Wildnerdpix/SS. **20:** CW craftsman/SS. **21:** Alex Cimbal/SS. **22:** Joel Everard/SS; pointbreak/SS. **23:** Alex Mit/SS; Olha1981/SS; Breedfoto/SS.**24:** Roy Pedersen/SS; SorbyPhoto/SS; infinetsoft/SS; Leonidas Santana/SS; Filip Bjorkman/SS; Morgan Worthington/SS. **25:** msgrafixx/SS; silky/SS; Dudarev Mikhail/SS. **26:** UnknownLatitude Images/SS; mark higgins/SS; freedomnaruk/SS. **27:** Geoscience Australia. **28:** NASA. **29:** EZ-Stock Studio/SS; Tsekhmister/SS; pizzastereo/SS. **30:** Saxon Vinkovic/SS; Milly Hooper. **31:** Vitaly Korovin/SS; MayaEmi/SS; Milly Hooper. **Back Cover:** Mim Cole.